SANDWICH SEARCH

Find and circle the names of sixteen types of sandwiches in the letters below. Look up, down, across, and backwards.

BOLOGNA
CHEESE
CHICKEN
CLUB   ROAST BEEF
FISH   SAUSAGE
HAM   STEAK
HAMBURGER   SUBMARINE
HOT DOG   TURKEY
MEATBALL
PASTRAMI
PEANUT BUTTER

```
N D L L A B T A E M P
N M R C Z L M B G H E
I B O L O G N A A H A
M H A M K J U T S S N
A O S B E H K G U I U
R T T U R K E Y A F T
T D B L L I G S S R B
S O E C V K A E T S U
A G E S E E H C O Z T
P O F N E K C I H C T
F S U B M A R I N E E
H A M B U R G E R D R
```

Illustrated by Lynn Adams

PROFESSOR HINK PINK

Professor Hink Pink likes to study things that rhyme. Here he is, doing a handstand in his fruit suit. Every payday, he takes time to find another rhyme. How many do you know in the picture below?

Answer on page 47.

IT'S A DIRTY JOB

Darian put a very unusual new laundry chute in his house. See if you can move Darian's sock through the chute to the laundry basket in the basement without getting stuck.

IN

OUT

Answer on page 47.

WOLFER AGNERD

If you unscramble WOLFER AGNERD, you'll find a beautiful FLOWER GARDEN. The scrambled words below are all flower names. How many do you know? Unscramble them in the spaces below each picture.

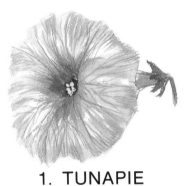

1. TUNAPIE

_____

2. FLODFAID

_____

3. SAYID

_____

4. SIIR

_____

5. PLUIT

_____

6. ERSO

_____

7. GLAMORID

_____

8. PYPOP

_____

Illustrated by George Fryer

Answer on page 47.

BATTER UP!

Step up to the plate and take a swing at this baseball crossword.

ACROSS

4. A one-base hit
6. The opposite of infield
10. A runner must touch each _____.
11. The person who calls out "Strike!"
14. A three-base hit
16. The player behind the plate
17. Nine players make a _____.
19. A scoring play
21. A batted ball that lands safely
22. The suit a player wears on the field

DOWN

1. The catcher's face protector
2. "Ball four" earns a _____ to first base.
3. The area inside the diamond
5. The ball is caught with a mitt or a _____.
7. A two-base hit
8. A four-base hit would be a _____ run.
9. A ball that is hit out of play
12. The player on the mound
13. The batter stands next to home _____.
15. The person who tries to hit the ball
16. The team's instructor
18. Three strikes
20. Number of innings in a normal game.

Answer on page 47.

ROW, ROW, ROW

Each doll has something in common with the two others in the same row. The dollmaker put the same hat on all three dolls in the top row across. Look at the other rows across, down, and diagonally. What's the same about each row of three?

Answer on page 48.

Illustrated by John Bennett

MAPPY LANDINGS

Three pilots flew over the states, landing at airports shown by the dots on this map. The lists below tell which states each pilot visited. Connect the dots for each route to show each pilot's path. Then look at the lines you've drawn to see where *all* of them were flying.

Pilot #1
Washington
Nevada
California
Arizona
Utah
Montana

Pilot #2
Minnesota
North Dakota
Wyoming
Iowa
Oklahoma
New Mexico

Pilot #3
Mississippi
New York
South Carolina
North Carolina
Tennessee

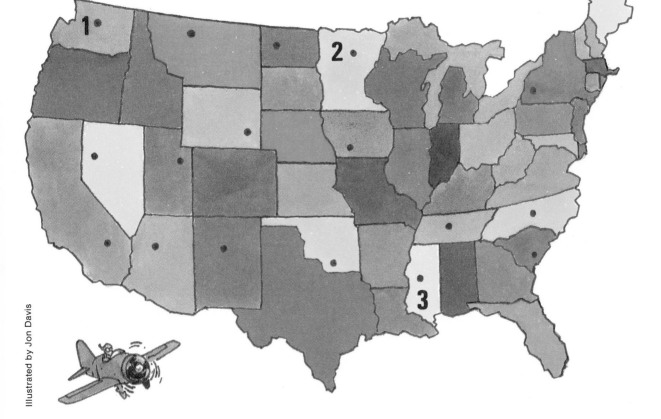

Illustrated by Jon Davis

SEE WHAT SUE SAW

Sue takes her binoculars wherever she goes. Can you tell where she went shopping each day?

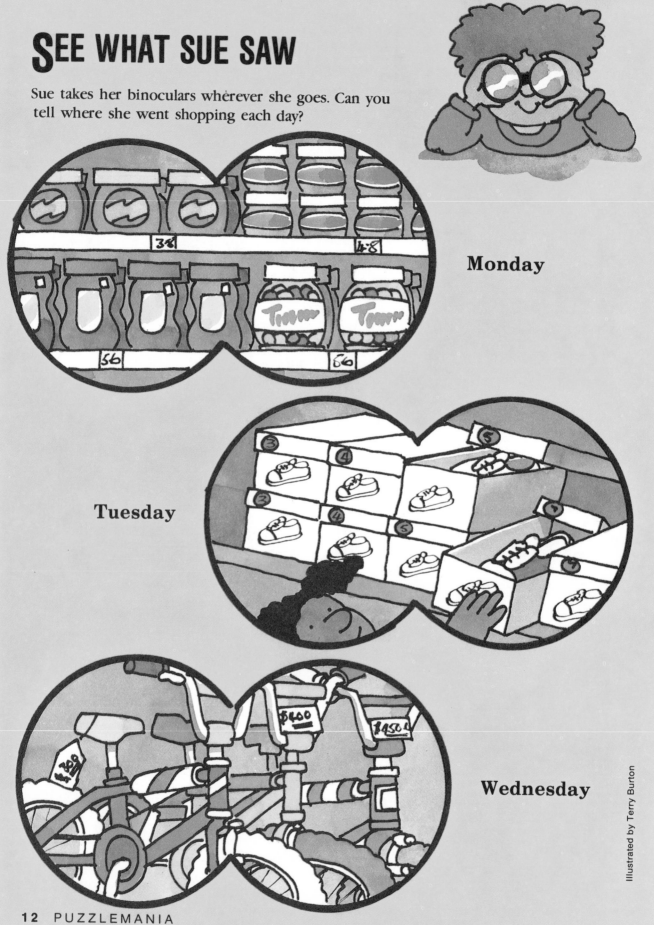

Monday

Tuesday

Wednesday

Thursday

Friday

Saturday

CATERPILLAR'S CAMERA

If caterpillars kept family scrapbooks, here are some pictures you might find inside. These pictures are out of order. Can you number them to show what happened first, second, and so on?

Illustrated by George Fryer

Answer on page 48.

JUNGLE REFLECTIONS

Other than things reflected upside down, there
are at least twelve differences between this scene
and its reflection. How many can you find?

Illustrated by Lynn Adams

IT'S ABOUT TIME

Copy these mixed-up squares in the spaces on the next page to put this picture back together. The letters and numbers tell you where each square belongs. The first one, A-3, has been done for you.

Illustrated by Rob Sepanak

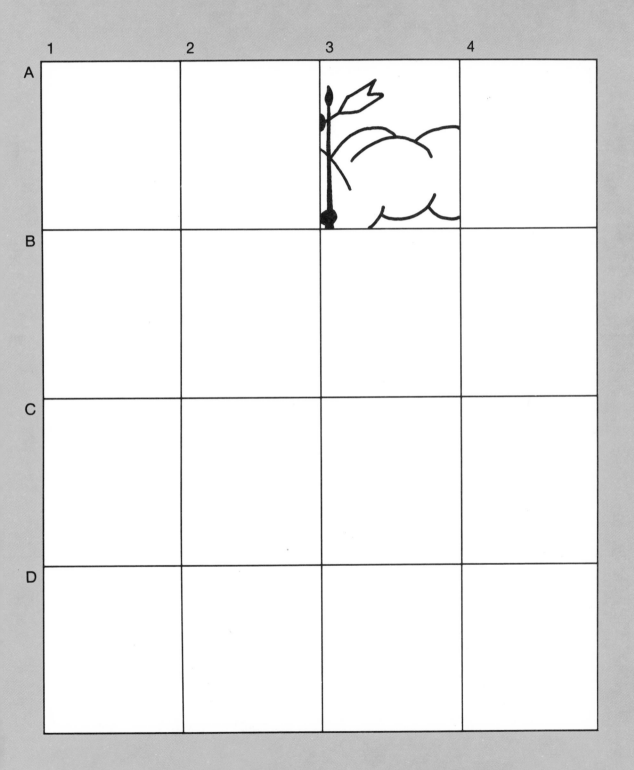

WHAT'S THE SCOOP?

Here's the menu at Shorty Shortcut's Ice-Cream Parlor. Can you read it?

1. BANA NA
2. ROOT BEER
3. CREAM
4. DIP DIP
5. MILK
6. CALENDAR / HOT FUDGE

Answer on page 48.

Illustrated by John Nez

BARNYARD MEMORIES

Take a long look at this picture. Try to remember everything you see in it. Then turn the page, and try to answer some questions about it without looking back.

Illustrated by Caroline Church

DON'T READ THIS UNTIL YOU HAVE LOOKED AT "Barnyard Memories—Part 1" ON PAGE 19.

BARNYARD MEMORIES
Part 2

Can you answer these questions about the barnyard scene you saw? Don't peek!

1. Was the barn door open or closed?
2. Which animal was drinking water?
3. How many horses were in the picture?
4. What animal was on the barn roof?
5. What color was the tractor?
6. What was the girl carrying?
7. Where did you see a bucket?
8. Was the tractor facing left or right?

Answer on page 48

COUNT UP!

Can you add up the numbers on these squares, circles, and triangles separately to find which shapes have the highest total and which shapes have the lowest?

Total ▢ _____
Total ◯ _____
Total ▲ _____

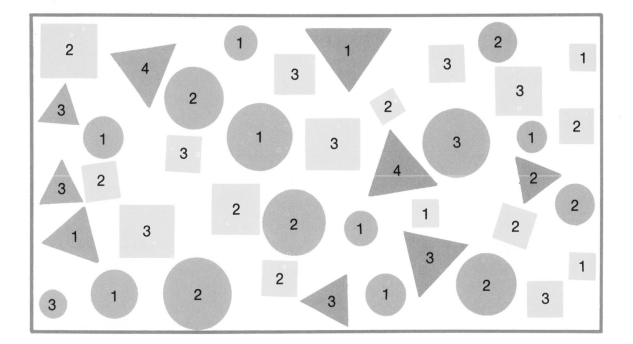

Answer on page 48.

WESTWORD HO!

Here are some words that may remind you of old cowboy movies. Find and circle the words in the letters below. Look up, down, across, backwards, and diagonally. Good luck, pardner!

BARN	BUNK	DOG	JEANS	RIDE
BIT	BUNKHOUSE	GUITAR	KERCHIEF	ROPE
BOOT	CAMP	HAT	MANE	SADDLE
BRAND	CHAPS	HAY	RANCH	WEST
BRONCO	CORRAL	HORSE	REIN	WHOA
BUCKING	COW			

```
T  S  E  W  Y  E  D  I  R  F
I  B  B  R  A  N  D  C  B  E
B  R  U  A  H  N  T  O  S  I
E  O  C  N  E  P  O  R  P  H
L  N  K  C  K  T  O  R  A  C
D  C  I  H  W  H  O  A  H  R
D  O  N  O  O  S  O  L  C  E
A  T  G  H  C  N  B  U  N  K
S  G  U  I  T  A  R  E  S  U
N  I  E  R  R  E  M  A  N  E
T  A  H  N  N  J  S  P  E  T
```

Leftover letter scramble: When you finish, write the uncircled letters in order in the spaces below. You'll find out where Cowboy Roy always rides to at the end of the movie.

I __ __ __ __   __ __ __   S __ __ __ __ __ __

Illustrated by John Nez

Answer on page 48.

TELL ME Y

Fourteen things on this page end in the letter Y. How many can you identify?

Answer on page 48.

Illustrated by Caroline Church

POLLY'S POCKETS

What's in Polly's pockets? Solve the clues, and move the numbered letters into the spaces at the bottom of the page. The answer may surprise you!

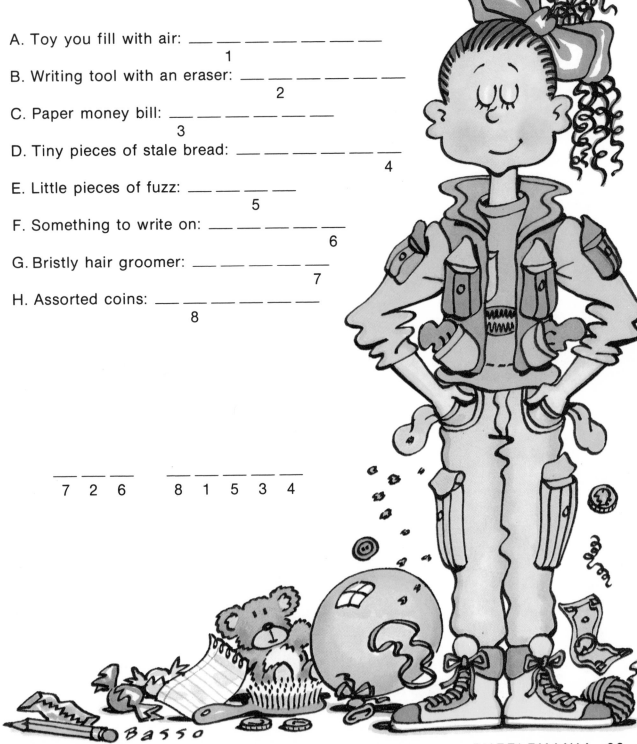

A. Toy you fill with air: __ __ __ __ __ __ __
                                           1

B. Writing tool with an eraser: __ __ __ __ __ __
                                        2

C. Paper money bill: __ __ __ __ __ __
                        3

D. Tiny pieces of stale bread: __ __ __ __ __ __ __
                                        4

E. Little pieces of fuzz: __ __ __ __ __
                          5

F. Something to write on: __ __ __ __ __
                              6

G. Bristly hair groomer: __ __ __ __ __
                            7

H. Assorted coins: __ __ __ __ __ __
                  8

__ __ __   __ __ __ __ __
7 2 6   8 1 5 3 4

Answer on page 49.

CROSSING THE OCEAN

These plants and animals all live in the ocean. Your challenge is to fit the words into the crisscrossing spaces. The lists tell how many letters are in each word. Some words have been filled in to get you started. When you have filled in a word, cross it off the list.

3 LETTERS
COD
EEL
RAY

4 LETTERS
BASS
CLAM
CRAB
SEAL
TUNA

5 LETTERS
ALGAE
CORAL
OTTER
SHARK
SQUID
WHALE

6 LETTERS
MARLIN
OYSTER
SALMON
SHRIMP
SPONGE
TURTLE
WALRUS

7 LETTERS
DOLPHIN
HADDOCK
HALIBUT
LOBSTER
OCTOPUS
SARDINE
SEAWEED
SUNFISH

8 LETTERS
BARNACLE
FLOUNDER
MACKEREL
PLANKTON
SAILFISH
SEAHORSE
STARFISH
STURGEON

9 LETTERS
ANGELFISH
BARRACUDA
JELLYFISH
SWORDFISH

Answer on page 49.

FIRST STAR I SEE TONIGHT

There are at least twelve differences between these two pictures. How many can you find?

Illustrated by Barbara Gray

INSTANT PICTURE

What's hidden on this page? To find out, fill in every
section that contains three dots.

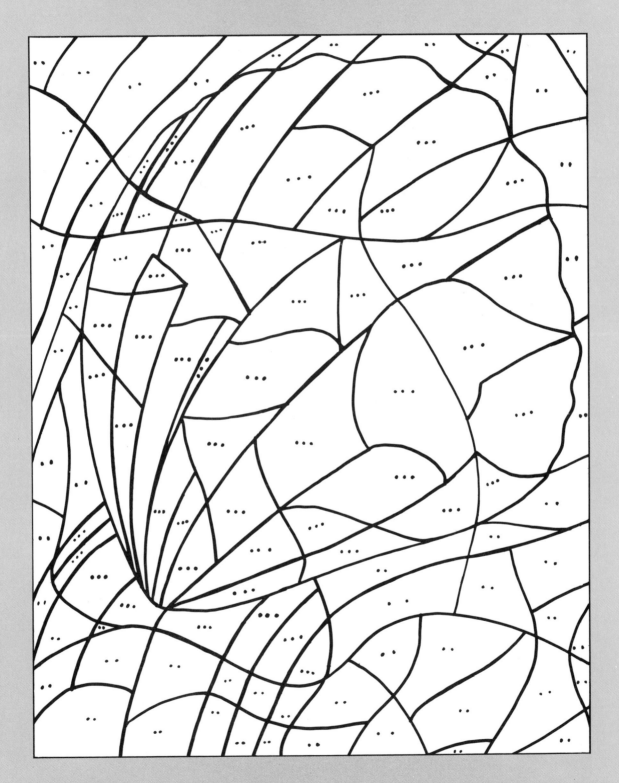

MITTEN MATCH

How many pairs of mittens can you find? Which mitten has no mate?

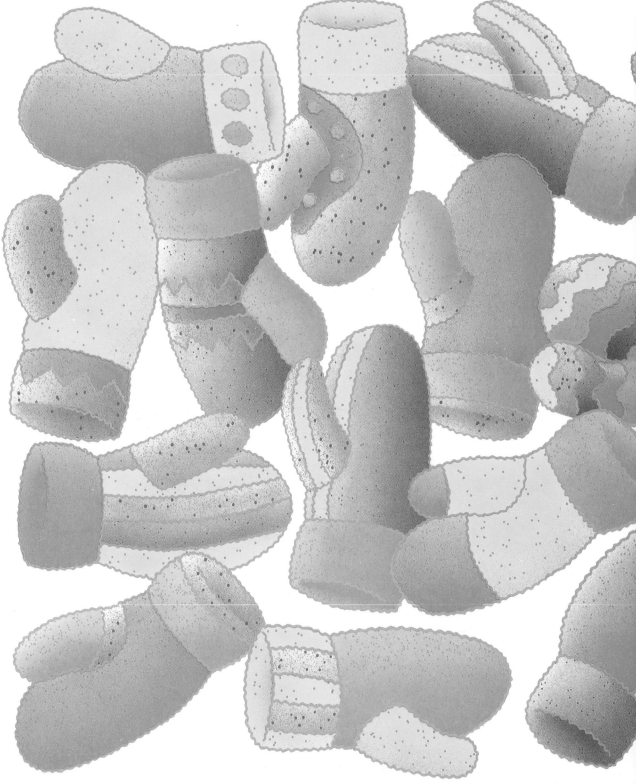

Answer on page 49.

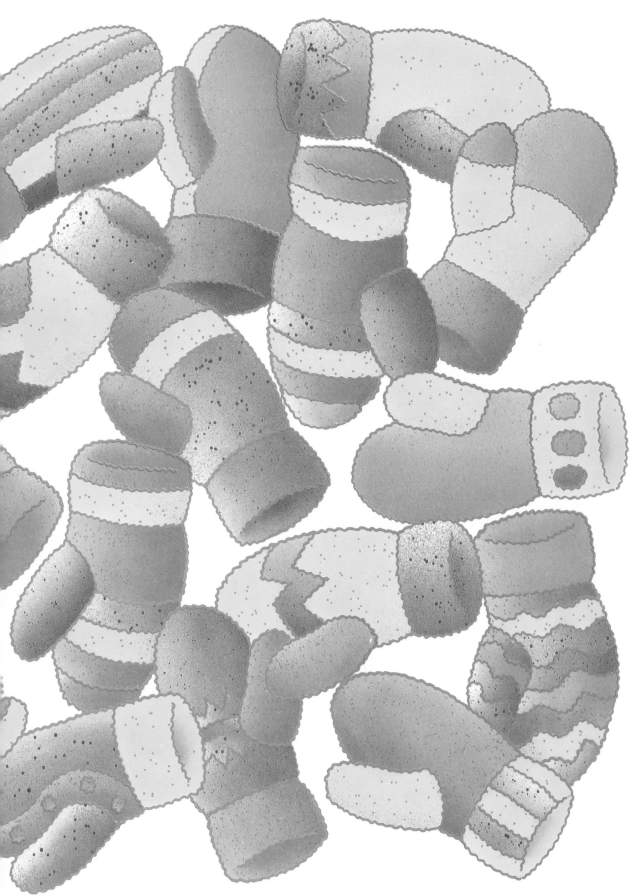

WHAT AM I?

I can travel all over the world for you, but I never get tired or complain.

I can travel by plane, ship, truck, or train.

I am carried places by men and women.

I am small and thin.

Sometimes I travel in a sack.

Sometimes I wear the face of a famous person like George Washington.

Sometimes I look like a flag or a mountain or a pretty bird.

I help deliver things.

When I get to my destination, I usually have ink on my face.

What am I?

Answer on page 49.

DOT MAGIC

Connect the dots to see where Cory would like to live.

HIDDEN PICTURES

There are at least 22 objects hidden in this picture. How many can you find?

Illustrated by Kit Wray

LEAF LOGIC

Jay, Ann, Emil, and Monica went hiking together. Each returned with a different leaf from one of the trees listed below. Use these clues to find out which hiker found which leaf.

Oak   Elm   Juniper   Magnolia

1. No one's name has the same number of letters as the name of the leaf he or she found.

2. No one found a leaf with the same first letter as his or her name.

Answer on page 49.

Illustrated by John Nez

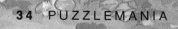

HAMMING IT UP

Using the clues below, see if you can make ten words that include the letters H-A-M. If you can, you're a real cHAMpion!

1. Tool used for pounding nails: H A M ___ ___ ___

2. Type of sweet cracker: ___ ___ ___ H A M

3. Container for dirty laundry: H A M ___ ___ ___

4. Hair washing fluid: ___ H A M ___ ___ ___

5. A favorite food at cookouts: H A M ___ ___ ___ ___ ___

6. Town where the Pied Piper played: H A M ___ ___ ___ ___

7. Bed that hangs between two trees: H A M ___ ___ ___ ___

8. Small, furry pet: H A M ___ ___ ___ ___

9. U.S. statesman on the $10 bill: H A M ___ ___ ___ ___ ___

10. One of the fifty states: ___ ___ ___   H A M ___ ___ ___ ___ ___

Answer on page 49.

BIG SECRETS

Use the secret number code to learn about a dinosaur and find out just how big it actually was.

___ ___ ___ ___ ___ ___ ___ ___ ___ ___ ___ ___ ___
2 18 1 3 8 9 15 19 1 21 18 21 19

was one of the ___ ___ ___ ___ ___ ___ ___ dinosaurs.
               2 9 7 7 5 19 20

It was about ___ ___ ___ ___ ___ ___ ___ — ___ ___ ___ ___
            19 5 22 5 14 20 25   6 9 22 5

feet long, and could reach the ___ ___ ___ ___ of the tallest
                             20 15 16 19

___ ___ ___ ___ ___ . This dinosaur had a long ___ ___ ___ ___ ___
20 18 5 5 19   19 14 15 21 20

with peg-like ___ ___ ___ ___ ___ .
             20 5 5 20 8

Illustrated by Belinda Lyon

A=1 B=2 C=3 D=4 E=5 F=6 G=7 H=8 I=9 J=10

K=11 L=12 M=13 N=14 O=15 P=16 Q=17 R=18 S=19 T=20

U=21 V=22 W=23 X=24 Y=25 Z=26

This gigantic __ __ __ __ __ __ __ __ was so
           4 9 14 15 19 1 21 18

__ __ __ __ __ that it had to __ __ __ all day in order
12 1 18 7 5   5 1 20

to get __ __ __ __ __ __ food. If it were __ __ __ __ __
       5 14 15 21 7 8   1 12 9 22 5

today, and stretched its __ __ __ __ upward, it could __ __ __ __
                         14 5 3 11   12 15 15 11

over the __ __ __ __ of a four-__ __ __ __ __
         18 15 15 6   19 20 15 18 25

__ __ __ __ __ __ __ __ . When you __ __ __ __ __ __ __ ,
 2 21 9 12 4 9 14 7   19 20 1 14 4 21 16

how __ __ __ can you see?
     6 1 18

Answer on page 49.

PUZZLEMANIA 37

WALKING THE HOG

These people are taking their pets on a walk. Follow the leashes to see which pet belongs to which person.

1.

A.

2.

B.

C.

D.

3.

4.

Answer on page 49.

Illustrated by Terry Burton

THE SNIGGLEDIP

Use your imagination, and draw the Sniggledip.

The Sniggledip's a silly creature
Made of silly things.
Its eyes look just like frying pans.
Its legs are like two springs.
Its nose is one long garden hose.
Its teeth are sharp as tacks.
But don't be scared —
It only likes asparagus for snacks.

Illustrated by Stephanie Longfoot

CRAZY CAR WASH

How many things can you find wrong in this picture?

Illustrated by Terry Rogers

BREAK TIME

Shana and Kate are looking for broken circles. How many will they find in the artwork on the wall? Look carefully!

Answer on page 50.

ANIMAL BABIES

What do you call a baby cow? A calf, of course. Look at each picture, and fill in the name of the animal's baby in the crossword puzzle.

ACROSS

DOWN

Illustrated by Teresa O'Brien

WHAT DOES IT ALL MEAN?

People around the world have their own languages.
These languages have words for things which are
different from their English names. See if you can
translate these foreign words.

1. *Danke* is a German word meaning . . .
    a. flowers
    b. handkerchief
    c. thank you

2. *Sayonara* is the Japanese word for . . .
    a. dress
    b. goodbye
    c. spaghetti

3. A Spanish boy would call his pet a *gatto* if it were
a . . .
    a. dog
    b. cat
    c. goldfish

4. To a French girl, a *chapeau* is a . . .
   a. hat
   b. tree
   c. house

5. *Nihow* is the Chinese word for . . .
   a. octopus
   b. knee socks
   c. hello

6. When an Italian says *prego,* it means . . .
   a. please
   b. rug
   c. excuse me

Answer on page 50.

STOP, LOOK, AND LIST

Under each category list one thing that begins with each letter. For example, one city that begins with "G" is Gary. See if you can name another.

AMERICAN CITIES

G_____

E_____

A_____

R_____

S_____

MOVIE TITLES

G_____

E_____

A_____

R_____

S_____

SCHOOL SUBJECTS

G_____

E_____

A_____

R_____

S_____

Illustrated by Lisa Dayer

Answer on page 50.

ANSWERS

COVER
Frogs number 2 and 7 are identical.

SANDWICH SEARCH (page 3)

PROFESSOR HINK PINK (pages 4-5)

Around Professor Hink Pink you will see:
Square hair
Bunny money
A clock lock
A pig wig
A cookbook
A star car
A fish dish
A mouse house
A pie tie
An ant's pants
A pink drink
A whale scale
A flower shower
A bat hat
A letter sweater
A red bed
A fat cat
A loose goose
A heart cart
A skate plate

IT'S A DIRTY JOB (page 6)

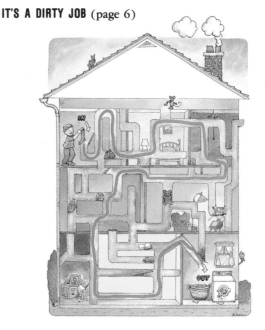

WOLFER AGNERD (page 7)

1. Petunia
2. Daffodil
3. Daisy
4. Iris

5. Tulip
6. Rose
7. Marigold
8. Poppy

BATTER UP! (pages 8-9)

ROW, ROW, ROW (page 10)

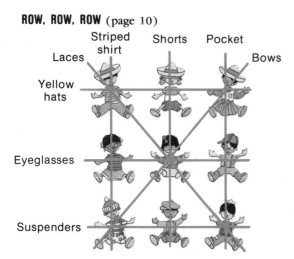

Laces — Striped shirt — Yellow hats — Shorts — Pocket — Bows — Eyeglasses — Suspenders

MAPPY LANDINGS (page 11)

SEE WHAT SUE SAW (page 12)
Monday: Grocery Store
Tuesday: Shoe Store
Wednesday: Bicycle Shop
Thursday: Fish Market
Friday: Book Store
Saturday: Flower Shop

CATERPILLAR'S CAMERA (page 14)
4   1
3   5
6   2

PICTURE MIXER (page 16-17)

WHAT'S THE SCOOP? (page 18)
1. Banana split
2. Root beer float
3. Ice cream
4. Double dip
5. Milk shake
6. Hot fudge sundae

BARNYARD MEMORIES (page 20)
1. Open
2. Cow
3. One
4. Cat
5. Red
6. A bag of corn
7. On the ground
8. Right

COUNT UP! (page 20)
The square numbers add up to thirty-eight, the circles add up to twenty-five, while the triangles are low with twenty-four.

WESTWORD HO! (page 21)

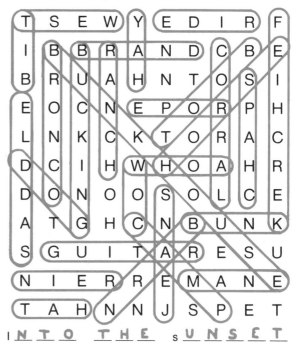

INTO THE SUNSET

TELL ME Y (page 22)
Butterfly
Pony
Cherry
Turkey
Chimney
Boy
Strawberry
Key
Candy
Baby
Donkey
Daisy
Monkey
Fly

POLLY'S POCKETS (page 23)

A. balloon
B. pencil
C. dollar
D. crumbs
E. lint
F. paper
G. brush
H. change

What's in Polly's pockets? Her hands.

CROSSING THE OCEAN (page 24-25)

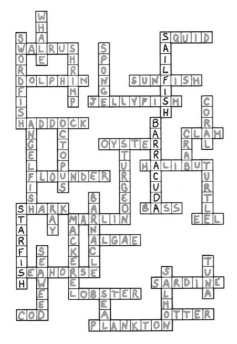

INSTANT PICTURE (page 27)

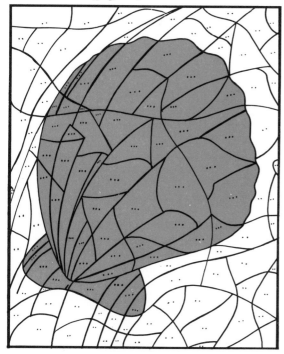

MITTEN MATCH (page 28-29)

There are 13 pairs of mittens.

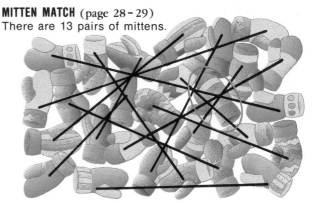

The one leftover mitten is circled above.

WHAT AM I? (page 30)

A stamp.

DOT MAGIC (page 31)

LEAF LOGIC (page 34)

Jay found the magnolia leaf, Ann has the juniper leaf, Emil picked up the oak leaf, and Monica found the elm leaf.

HAMMING IT UP (page 35)

1. Hammer
2. Graham
3. Hamper
4. Shampoo
5. Hamburger
6. Hamelin
7. Hammock
8. Hamster
9. Hamilton
10. New Hampshire

BIG SECRETS (page 36-37)

Brachiosaurus was one of the **biggest** dinosaurs. It was about **seventy-five** feet long, and could reach the **tops** of the tallest **trees.** This dinosaur had a long **snout** with peg-like **teeth.**

This gigantic **dinosaur** was so **large** that it had to **eat** all day in order to get **enough** food. If it were **alive** today, and stretched its **neck** upward, it could **look** over the **roof** of a four-**story building.**

When you **stand up,** how **far** can you see?

WALKING THE HOG (page 38)

1. C, 2. D, 3. B, 4. A